VIVARI.

-th America

AMERICAN BEAVERS

by Alicia Z. Klepeis

FOCUS
READERS

www.northstareditions.com

Produced for North Star Editions by Red Line Editorial.

Photographs ©: Paul Reeves Photography/Shutterstock Images, cover, 1; stanley45/iStockphoto, 4–5; NancyS/Shutterstock Images, 7; Red Line Editorial, 8; Martin Janca/Shutterstock Images, 10–11; Gail Johnson/Shutterstock Images, 13; Oleksandr Lytvynenko/Shutterstock Images, 15, 29; Johannes Dag Mayer/Shutterstock Images, 16–17; David Fossler/Shutterstock Images, 19; photographybyJHWilliams/iStockphoto, 20–21, 27 (bottom left); robertcicchetti/iStockphoto, 22–23; UbjsP/Shutterstock Images, 24, 27 (bottom right); Little_Things/Thinkstock, 27 (top)

ISBN
978-1-63517-028-3 (hardcover)
978-1-63517-084-9 (paperback)
978-1-63517-187-7 (ebook pdf)
978-1-63517-137-2 (hosted ebook)

Library of Congress Control Number: 2016951026

Printed in the United States of America
Mankato, MN
November, 2016

About the Author

Alicia Z. Klepeis began her career at the National Geographic Society. She loves to research fun and out-of-the-ordinary topics that make nonfiction exciting for readers. Alicia is the author of numerous children's books including *The World's Strangest Foods*, *Bizarre Things We've Called Medicine*, *A Time for Change*, and *Francisco's Kites*.

TABLE OF CONTENTS

CHAPTER 1

NEED FOR TREES

Near a wooded pond, a beaver digs its long teeth into a tree's bark. In minutes, the beaver chomps its way through the tree.

Beavers use trees and branches to build their dams and homes.

Beavers live in forested areas where lots of trees grow. They use trees to build their homes.

Beavers also eat trees. They are **herbivores**. They munch tree bark, leaves, and twigs. Beavers also eat **cambium**. This soft tissue grows beneath the bark of a tree.

FUN FACT

A beaver's teeth grow throughout the animal's life. Chewing wood prevents their teeth from becoming too long.

A beaver swims while eating water lilies.

In warmer weather, beavers have more variety in their diet. They eat plants that grow in the water, such as water lilies. They also eat plant roots, grass, ferns, fruit, and seeds.

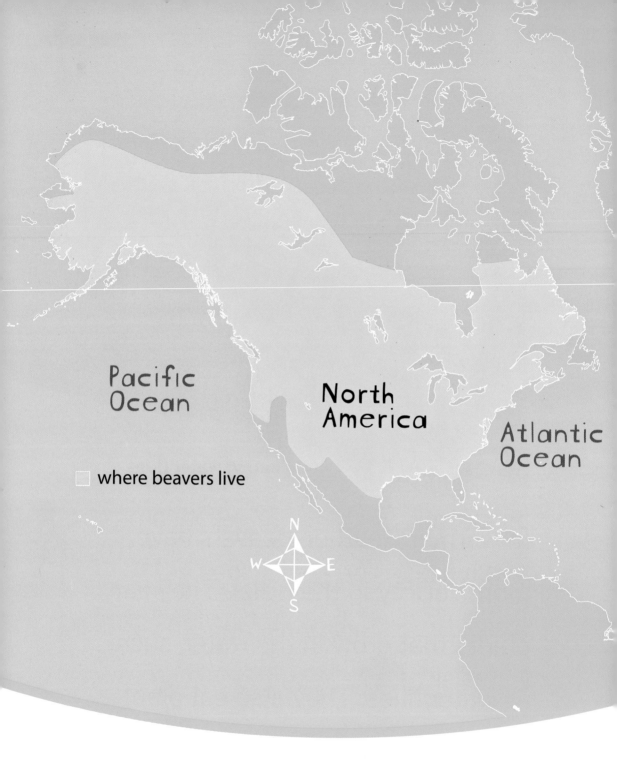

Pacific
Ocean

North
America

Atlantic
Ocean

☐ where beavers live

N
W E
S

Beavers live in most parts of North America.

Beavers are nocturnal. This means they are most active at night.

Beavers make their homes near rivers, streams, lakes, ponds, and marshes. Making a home in the water helps protect beavers from **predators** such as coyotes, bears, and lynx. If a predator does get too close, beavers can dive into the water and swim to safety.

CHAPTER 2

MADE FOR WATER

Special **adaptations** make life in the water easier for beavers. **Watertight** flaps of skin seal off their ears and nostrils. Beavers can also pull their lips behind their teeth.

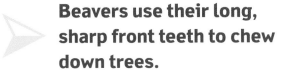

Beavers use their long, sharp front teeth to chew down trees.

This allows them to carry objects and chew wood while underwater without gulping water. Their front paws are good for picking up sticks and mud. Their claws work great for digging. They can cut down trees with their big front teeth.

FUN FACT

Beavers have clear eyelids that let them see underwater while also protecting their eyes. The eyelids act as swim goggles.

▷ Beavers also use their long teeth to hold and carry large branches.

Beavers' webbed hind feet help them swim. They use their broad, flat tails to steer when swimming. Beavers also use their tails to communicate.

They slap their tails on the water to warn other beavers of danger.

Beavers are **mammals**. Two layers of fur help keep beavers warm. Beavers have special **glands** under their tails that make an oily substance. They rub this substance over their fur to make it waterproof.

FUN FACT

Beavers can swim at a speed of approximately 5 miles per hour (8.0 km/h).

PARTS OF AN AMERICAN BEAVER

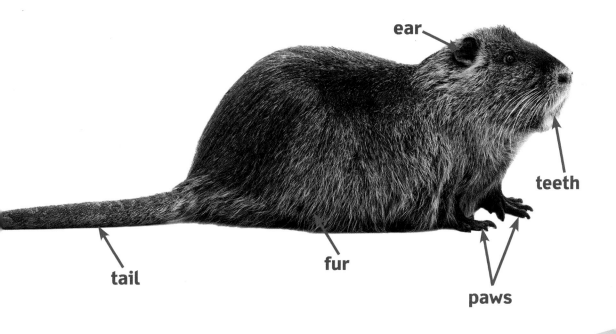

ear

teeth

fur

paws

tail

Beavers often measure more than 3 feet (0.9 m) long, including the tail. An adult beaver can weigh 60 pounds (27 kg).

CHAPTER 3

DAMS AND WATER LODGES

Beavers build dams across streams, rivers, and lakes. They use their sharp teeth to cut down trees. Then they drag the logs and branches into the water and float them to the dam site.

Without dams, beavers' homes might get washed away.

The trees pile up and block the flow of water. Beavers use broken branches, mud, and stones to make their dams watertight. A dam creates a pond where the beavers can build their home.

After building a dam, beavers create dome-shaped homes. These are called lodges. The lodge's living space is above the water's surface. That keeps it dry inside. The lodge has an air hole at the top. The hole lets fresh

> Beavers use branches, mud, and stone to make lodges.

air in for the beavers to breathe.
The entrance to the lodge is
underwater. This keeps predators
from entering.

THE WORLD'S BIGGEST BEAVER DAM

Sometimes beaver families work together to build large beaver dams. The largest beaver dam in the world is in Alberta, Canada. This dam is located in the Wood Buffalo National Park. Beavers started the dam in 1975. The dam measures 2,790 feet (850 m) in length. It is so big that it can be seen from space!

The beaver dam in Alberta, Canada, was constructed like all other beaver dams but on a much larger scale.

CHAPTER 4

COLONIES AND KITS

Beavers are social animals. They live with their families. These groups are called colonies. Members of each colony work and play together all year round.

Baby beavers are called kits.

> **Kits stay near their mother.**

Beavers start mating when they are approximately three years old. Female beavers usually have

Kits can swim within 24 hours of birth.

one **litter** every spring. There are usually between one and nine kits in a litter.

Both parents help take care of the kits. Kits stay with their parents for two winters. During the second winter, older beavers help with the new litter of kits.

In addition to watching the younger beavers, year-old beavers also help with other jobs. They might repair the lodge or dam, or they might gather food to store for winter. After the second winter, the young beavers leave the lodge. They go out to build lodges and start their own families.

FUN FACT

Beavers can stay underwater for up to 15 minutes.

AMERICAN BEAVER LIFE CYCLE

Kits are born in spring.

Kits stay with their mothers until they are just over two years old.

Young beavers go out to build their own lodges.

FOCUS ON
AMERICAN BEAVERS

Write your answers on a separate piece of paper.

1. Write a sentence that describes the key ideas from Chapter 2.

2. Do you think beavers have the best features to live in water? What other features might benefit beavers?

3. What is a group of beavers called?
   A. colony
   B. litter
   C. kit

4. How might beavers live differently if they didn't have watertight flaps of skin to seal off their ears and nostrils from water?
   A. They would not be able to hear or smell as well.
   B. They would not be able to dive underwater to get into their lodges.
   C. They would not be able to swim.

5. What does **communicate** mean in this book?

    A. to share information with movements

    B. to share information by talking

    C. to share information with eye contact

Beavers also use their tails to **communicate**. They slap their tails on the water to warn other beavers of potential dangers.

6. What does **social** mean in this book?

    A. living alone

    B. a gathering of people

    C. living with others

Beavers are **social** animals. They live with their families.

Answer key on page 32.

GLOSSARY

adaptations
Changes in an animal or its body parts that make it better suited to its environment.

cambium
A thin cell layer of plants from which new cells, such as wood and bark, develop.

glands
Organs in the body that produce chemicals used by other parts of the body.

herbivores
Animals that eat mostly plants.

litter
A group of young born to an animal at one time.

mammals
Animals that give birth to live babies, have fur or hair, and produce milk.

predators
Animals that kill and eat other animals.

watertight
So tight that water cannot get through.

TO LEARN MORE

BOOKS

Gish, Melissa. *Beavers*. Mankato, MN: Creative Education, 2015.

Hinman, Bonnie. *Keystone Species That Live in Ponds, Streams, and Wetlands*. Hockessin, DE: Mitchell Lane Publishers, 2016.

Wilson, Emily. *Inside Beaver Lodges*. New York: PowerKids Press, 2015.

NOTE TO EDUCATORS

Visit **www.focusreaders.com** to find lesson plans, activities, links, and other resources related to this title.

INDEX

Answer Key: **1.** Answers will vary; **2.** Answers will vary; **3.** A; **4.** B; **5.** A; **6.** C